Love That Doesn't Hurt

From Trauma to Trust: Relearning Love After
Narcissistic Abuse

Genevieve McPartlin-Bryant

Dedication

For my husband.

For showing me that love can be safe.

For being patient with the walls, you didn't build.

For holding space for the version of me that was still learning to trust.

You loved me through undoing, through the healing, and into the light.

You never asked me to be anything but myself – and somehow, that made me everything.

This book – this part of me – exists because of the way you love me.

You are proof that love doesn't have to hurt.

Always yours.

Before Love Found Me

I used to think love was supposed to ache.

That butterflies meant fear, not excitement.

That proving my worth was part of being chosen.

I didn't realize I was chasing the ghosts of my past —

Men who looked like comfort only because they mirrored the chaos I came from.

I said "I'm fine" a lot.

I confused being needed with being loved.

I tolerated more than I ever should have,

Because deep down, I didn't believe I deserved more.

I wanted to be held, but I flinched when someone reacted for me.

I wanted to be loved, but I didn't trust anyone who didn't make me fight for it.

I didn't know what soft love felt like —

Because all I'd known was sharp edges and conditional care.

I thought that was love.

Until I started healing.

Until I realized that love isn't supposed to hurt,

And I am allowed to rewrite what it looks like now.

Acknowledgements

This book would not exist without the pain that shaped me, the healing that saved me, and the people who stood beside me through both.

To my husband – thank you for loving me with a steady hand and a patient heart. For showing me that love can be soft, honest, and safe. For reminding me, every single day, that I am not too much – I was just waiting for the right person to see me fully. You are that person, and you always will be.

To the readers – especially the ones who see themselves in these pages. I wrote this for you. For the little version of you who needed someone to say, "I believe you." For the grown version who's still learning that healing is not a straight line, but a brave one.

And finally, to the girl I used to be – I'm so proud of you for surviving. And I'm even more proud that you never stopped hoping for more.

Table of Contents:

Part I:

The Wounds We Carried

Chapter 1:

The Ghosts We Date

We don't always fall in love with people.

Sometimes, we fall in love with patterns.

With wounds that feel familiar.

With chaos that feels like home.

When you grow up in a world where love was conditional, manipulative, or unpredictable, your body starts to believe that's just how love works. So when someone enters your life who gives you butterflies and keeps you guessing, it doesn't feel like danger – it feels like love.

I chased those ghosts for years. Men who mimicked my father's inconsistencies. People who knew how to pull me in, then punish me for getting close. I didn't realize I was reenacting the same emotional abandonment over and over – I just thought I had bad luck with relationships.

Looking back, it's almost haunting. I can see the signs now. The way I craved attention, not affection. The way I mistook anxiety for chemistry. The way I clung to anyone who mirrored the emotional distance I had grown up with – because deep down, I believed if I could finally get *them* to love me… maybe I'd finally be enough.

We date the ghost of who hurt us, hoping this time we'll get it right.

But love isn't a test you have to pass.

It's not a prize you earn for suffering enough.

It's not supposed to feel like waiting to be chosen.

And yet – for so long – I thought It was.

At the time, I thought I was just falling in love.

But now I can see I was trying to impress someone else entirely

\-   *My father*

Somewhere deep down, I think I believed that if I brought home someone who resembled him – emotionally, or even just in attitude – maybe he'd finally take an interest. Maybe he'd approve. Maybe if *he* liked the man I brought home, it would mean he liked *me* too.

It's twisted logic, I know. But when you grow up constantly trying to win someone's love, that hunger follows you into adulthood. I wasn't looking for a partner – I was chasing validation.

My father played the role of the "cool, protective dad," the one who'd joke that no man would ever be good enough for his daughter. But he didn't know me. Not really. He hadn't earned the right to be protective. This was a man who had to *double-check the date of his only daughter's birthday*. One of only two children – and he couldn't even remember the day I was born.

That line – "no one's good enough for you" – wasn't about protecting me. It was a mirror of how he felt about me. *I* wasn't good enough. That message was always there, just beneath the surface, in how he compared me to others, in how he withheld praise, in how he made me feel invisible.

But I didn't understand that yet. So, I kept trying.

I fell in love with emotionally unavailable men because I was trying to earn the love of an emotionally unavailable father. I brought home men who looked strong on the outside but made me feel small behind closed doors. Men who mirrored his manipulation, his withdrawal, his way of making everything feel like my fault.

Looking back, I don't think I was really in love with those men. I think I was just desperate to feel loved at all.

One of them didn't even wait for permission.

From the day we met, he inserted himself into my world like it was his to claim. He stayed, even when a small voice in me whispered that something felt off. And soon, that voice was silenced – drowned beneath the weight of control, fear, and the false security that I had mistaken for connection.

He made everything about power.

He controlled my appearance. My body. My weight. There were literal **weekly weigh-ins**, and if the number on the scale didn't reflect what he deemed acceptable, there were consequences – emotional, verbal, and psychological. I was no longer a person. I was a project. Something to mold. Something to own.

When we visited my family for the holidays, no one suspected a thing. I didn't feel safe enough to tell them what was really happening behind closed doors. He played the role of supporting partner so well. Charming. Attentive. Helpful. But that was all part of it – just like my father. The ego came first. The performance was polished. And what the world saw became more important than what I was enduring.

Behind closed doors, everything unraveled.

And I was close enough to be the number one target.

It took me years to realize that what I what I was living wasn't love – it was survival. And worse, I had mistaken survival for connection because I had never been taught the difference. The emotional blueprint I was given was so warped that even cruelty looked familiar. Even control felt like care. Even fear…felt like love.

And here's the hardest part to admit:

I didn't think I deserved better.

I thought I had to earn softness. I thought calm was suspicious.

I thought being treated well meant the other shoe was just waiting to drop.

And when you've never known safe love…

You start to believe it doesn't exist.

I See You

If any part of this feels familiar —

I want you to know something right now:

You are not overreacting.

You are not being dramatic.

You are not too sensitive.

And you are *not alone*.

If you've ever silenced your instincts to keep the peace…

If you've ever been loved with conditions…

If you've ever doubted your worth because of the way someone treated you, —

I see you.

I was you.

And I promise, love that doesn't hurt *is real*.

You just haven't been taught how to recognize it yet.

But that's what we're going to do together.

Journal Reflection:

I am allowed to unlearn the love I thought I deserved.

I am allowed to question patterns I once called home.

I am allowed to stop chasing approval that was never mine to earn.

The pain I've lived does not make me unworthy of love –

It makes me more attuned to what love *should* be.

I don't have to know what safe love looks like yet.

I only must believe it exists.

And I am learning.

One truth at a time.

Chapter 2:

We Thought That Was Normal

We didn't know it was abuse.

We didn't know it was control.

We didn't know that real love doesn't feel like anxiety.

Because it was *all we ever knew.*

There's something heartbreaking about looking back and realizing the things that made you flinch… were the same things you were taught to call *love.*

The yelling.

The guilt trips.

The silent treatment.

The walking-on-eggshells feeling that lived in your chest like a second heartbeat.

You told yourself it was normal – because it had to be. Because otherwise, it meant your childhood wasn't safe. And that truth is too heavy for a child to carry.

So, we tell ourselves stories. We make excuses.

"This is just how relationships are."

"They act this way because they care."

"This is love – I just have to work harder to deserve it."

And when you grow up with that kind of conditioning, it becomes your default setting.

So, you find yourself in adult relationships tolerating emotional neglect, brushing off red flags, or second-guessing your own boundaries – because deep down, the love you were shown trained you to believe that **you are the problem.**

We were told things like:

"Boys are mean to you because they like you."

"He's just jealous."

"That's how people show they care."

Simple phrases, said with a shrug... but each one teaching us to question our instincts and excuse harm.

I hear those lines often. As a child, I didn't have the language for what I was feeling, but I knew something didn't sit right. I just didn't feel safe. But instead of being validated, I was told I was *too sensitive, too emotional,* or *reading too much into things.*

So, I started to believe it was my fault.

Even worse were adults who tried to explain away my father's behavior.

"He loves you. He just doesn't know how to show it."

Really?

Because when he moved across the country and left his young children behind… it didn't feel like love. When he ignored my accomplishments but showed up for everyone else's… it didn't feel like love. When he made me feel like a burden for just having needs, it didn't feel like love.

And when people told me, *"He does it because he loves you,"* it didn't comfort me.

It confused me.

It made me question my pain.

It taught me that maybe love is supposed to feel like being abandoned, criticized, or even hit.

That's how the pattern begins.

Not just in our childhoods, but in our minds.

Love doesn't hit.

Love doesn't manipulate.

Love doesn't disappear when it's inconvenient.

But when we're told it does – over and over – we learn to settle for pain that feels familiar instead of love that feels safe.

And sometimes, it's not even the loud harm that sticks with you – it's the silence that followed it.

The lack of apology.

The absence of accountability.

Growing up, I was never really taught that adults make mistakes. In my world, parents didn't say, "I'm sorry." They didn't own up to the ways they hurt us – emotionally, physically, or otherwise. They pretended it didn't happen. Or worse, they twisted it into something *we* did wrong.

"You're just being dramatic."

"I didn't mean it like that."

"You're too sensitive."

The emotional immaturity was disguised as strength. But all it ever really taught me was that love doesn't say sorry – and that I shouldn't expect it to.

My father was a master manipulator. He had a way of presenting "help" like a gift, but the gift always came with strings. If he paid for something, it was never just an act of generosity – it became leverage.

A tool to guilt me.

A reminder that I owed him.

A reason to remind me that he was the one in control.

And for a long time, I didn't question it. I accepted it. Because I had been conditioned to see that kind of treatment as love. I didn't know better. I thought it was normal.

I See You

If no one ever apologized to you…

If you were taught that your pain was inconvenient…

If love came with conditions, guilt, or silence –

I want you to hear this now:

You were never asking for too much.

You were asking for *basic emotional safety.*

And I know how hard it is to unlearn what you were raised to believe…

But love is not supposed to make you feel small.

Love does not make you feel like a burden.

Love does not hand you gifts just to use them as weapons later.

Love is safe.

Love is soft.

Love says, "I'm sorry. I hurt you. I want to do better."

Even if no one showed you that growing up –

You are allowed to expect it now.

Journal Reflection:

I am allowed to question the version of love I was taught.

I am allowed to expect accountability, softness, and care.

I am allowed to stop mistaking silence for strength.

I don't owe anyone a lifetime of loyalty just because they offered me help.

I am no longer available for love that comes with guilt.

I am worthy of love that says,

"I'm sorry I hurt you... and I will do better."

Chapter 3:

Red Flags We Called Romance

They didn't come waving red flags.

They came carrying flowers.

Saying all the right things.

Making us feel like the center of the universe.

And that's what made it so hard to leave.

When you've been starved of emotional connection, the *bare minimum* can feel magical. The smallest gestures – morning texts, complements, attention – can light you up like you've finally been chosen. And if someone shoers you with affection early on, you don't see it as a warning… you see it as everything you've ever wanted.

Because no one ever taught us what love was supposed to look like.

We learned from experience – and those experiences weren't safe. So, when love came rushing in fast and loud, we mistook the chaos for passion. The obsession for romance. The control for protection.

What we didn't know was that love bombing is real.

That manipulation often comes dressed in charm.

That abusive people are often masters at making you feel special before making you feel trapped.

I met someone not long after I moved to Texas. We had connected through an app, and everything about him *seemed* perfect – smart, well-educated, charming. He messaged like a gentleman. Told me how beautiful I was. Said all the right things.

I was barely 18.

He was 24.

I hadn't yet had a real relationship – not one I chose, not one where I had control. My first sexual experience had been taken from me when I was 14, and in the years since, I had avoided anything intimate. I wasn't ready.

Maybe that's what drew him to me. I was young. Inexperienced. Unsure of what *normal* was. The perfect target.

He didn't pressure me at first. That's what made him feel safe. We talked for a while before we met in person. And when we did… it was easy to fall. He was smooth. He made me feel chosen. Special. I didn't realize he had crafted the illusion for exactly that purpose.

It became my first "real" experience. And I believed it was love. But we weren't *together*. We were… something. On his terms. He saw me when it was convenient. He called when he wasn't "too busy."

Every time we spent together, it ended the same way: physical. Not emotional. Not vulnerable. Just convenient for *him*.

I told myself it was normal. That it was casual. That maybe he just needed time.

But I was lying to myself – because I was already in love with him.

I confessed my feelings once. He dodged it. Avoided giving it a name.

I broke it off eventually… but I went back. Just like so many of us do.

He invited me to a friend's wedding and made me feel like it meant something.

That maybe this was a sign we were finally real.

But it wasn't about us – it was about appearances. He wanted someone pretty on his arm.

Something extra for the night. Not a relationship. Not care. Not me.

I ended it for good.

And about a year later, I met my husband. We got engaged quickly – and you know who showed up again?

Mr. Seems Perfect but Hides a Deeper Motive.

Because when someone's love is performative, not genuine – they only come back when they lose control. When they can't have you anymore.

That wasn't love.

That was manipulation dipped in attention.

That was control disguised as romance.

That was emotional power play masked as chemistry.

I See You

If you've ever found yourself falling for someone who made you feel high… then hollow —

If you've confused attention for affection…

If you've stayed too long, hoping this time it would finally turn into something real —

You are not naïve.

You are not broken.

You are not stupid for wanting to be loved.

You were vulnerable.

And someone exploited that vulnerability.

But your capacity to love deeply? That's not a weakness.

That's your superpower.

You deserve to give that love to someone who *chooses you back*.

Journal Reflection:

I no longer confuse chaos for confusion.

I see the red flags I used to call romance.

I release the belief that I must earn love by proving
my worth.

I am no longer impressed by grand gestures that
come with conditions.

I am drawn to peace now – consistency, safety,
slowness.

Love doesn't play games with my heart.

It meets me where I am.

And I will never again settle for someone who only
wants the parts of me that are easy to hold.

Chapter 4:

The Love That Broke Me

Not every heartbreak comes from someone walking away.

Sometimes, it comes from staying.

From surviving someone who smiled for the world —

But destroyed you behind closed doors.

This was the one that broke me.

I've talked about patterns. About red flags. About unhealthy love disguised as romance.

But this wasn't just emotionally abusive.

It was violent.

It was calculated.

It was terrifying.

I was in that relationship for close to a year, and with every month that passed, it got worse. More controlling. More manipulative. More dangerous. To everyone else, he played the part of a stable, attentive man. The one who smiled politely.

Charmed easily. Looked like someone you could trust.

But to me, he was a monster.

He fed off fear – especially mine. He took things I told him in confidence – my discomfort with medical providers, my triggers around certain environments, even weapons – and he used them as fuel. He didn't just hurt me. He *enjoyed* hurting me.

But the worst part wasn't just what he did to me.

It was how he used what I loved most to break me.

He knew I wanted to be a mother. He knew more than anything in this world, I wanted a baby. I had dreamed of it. I talked about it. It was my calling.

So, he used that too.

He refused protection.

Found and destroyed the pills I tried to take in secret.

Monitored my weight.

Forced weekly pregnancy tests – administered by *him*.

And when the two lines finally appeared, I knew. I had lost control over my own body.

Because this wasn't a shared joy.

It was a weapon.

We confirmed the pregnancy out-of-pocket. Quietly.

I didn't want my father's insurance involved — not in something *this sacred.*

I was carrying something beautiful inside me — something I wanted with every fiber of my being. But it was attached to someone who only saw it as another form of power.

About ten weeks in, we had one of our worst fights.

He kicked me. Repeatedly.

I fought back with everything I had — but more than anything, I fought to protect that baby.

I didn't know it then, but the trauma was already too much.

Later that night, I began bleeding. And he was gone.

I went to the nearest Planned Parenthood and paid in cash.

And that's where I learned the truth.

I had lost my baby.

My body had done what it had to do — abort the pregnancy to protect *me.*

A week later, the results from our gender test arrived in the mail.

It was a boy.

I stayed in that relationship for four more months.

That tells you everything you need to know about how broken I was.

I got out. Eventually.

And on the anniversary of the loss, I got a tattoo – two tiny baby feet on my ribs.

A quiet tribute to the boy I never got to hold.

And a silent promise to the girl I used to be...

That I would never, ever let myself be broken like that again.

This wasn't just heartbreak.

It was grief.

It was trauma.

It was a death of innocence.

And I carried the guilt like it was mine to bear.

I See You

If someone ever used your dreams as leverage –

If you stayed because you were too afraid to leave –

If you ever carried shame for something that wasn't your fault…

I want you to hear me now:

What happened to you wasn't love.

It was manipulation. It was abuse.

And you never deserved any part of it.

You didn't fail to protect yourself.

You survived the impossible.

And even if you still carry pieces of that pain…

You are *not* broken.

You are still worthy of joy.

You are still worthy of love.

And you are still here.

That is your power.

Journal Reflection:

I no longer carry guilt for the pain someone else caused.

I will not blame myself for what someone else chose to do.

I deserved to be loved, not used.

Cherished, not controlled.

Protected, not punished.

What I lost was not my fault.

What I carry now is not shame, but strength.

I am allowed to grieve what should have been.

And I am still worthy of the love I've always dreamed of.

I survived what tried to break me.

And I am still becoming whole.

Part II:
Relearning Love

Chapter 5:

Is this Love or Survival?

We spend years praying for a love that doesn't hurt.

And when it finally arrives – calm, consistent, safe –

It doesn't feel like love at all.

It feels like fear.

Because we've only ever known love with conditions.

Safe love isn't loud.

It doesn't come crashing into your life.

It doesn't feel like anxiety or adrenaline.

So, when someone finally treats you with care, when they don't raise their voice, when they don't punish you for your boundaries – your nervous system doesn't register it as *comfort*. It registers it as confusion.

Because trauma tells us love should be earned.

That we need to perform.

That if we're not anxious, we're not invested.

So, when we finally meet someone who doesn't want to fix us or change us or control us… we flinch.

We overthink.

We wait for the shift.

We test them, because it feels safer to push them away than risk being let down.

Safe love doesn't feel the way you expect it to.

It doesn't rush in like a tidal wave.

It doesn't demand.

It doesn't pull fireworks from the sky.

It's quiet.

Patient.

Steady.

And if you've been raised to see love as something you must *earn* – that kind of calm can feel deeply unsettling.

When my husband reached out to me, I was in a chapter of life where I'd sworn off dating. I had just begun rebuilding after everything I'd been through. I was a single mom – to a son from a different relationship – focused on creating a life that *didn't revolve around being chosen.*

We already knew each other – grew up in the same small town, went to school together. But this was years later. He reached out through Instagram DMs. And I immediately felt myself freeze.

Because I had learned that love starts like this.

With attention. With flattery. With charm.

And then… it changes.

It turns.

So, I rejected him. Not in a dramatic way – just quietly, gently.

I was scared.

Not because he did anything wrong.

But because I *knew* I could fall for him. And falling had always led to pain.

But here's what was different.

He didn't push.

He didn't disappear.

He didn't guilt me for saying no.

He stayed. Quietly. Kindly.

He messaged me almost every day. Never pressuring. Just… *being there.*

Six months passed before I agreed to meet him.

And when I did — it felt like something had clicked into place. Like my soul *recognized* something in him it had been waiting for all along.

Later, he asked me what made me hesitate at first.

And I told him the truth.

I wasn't afraid he'd hurt me.

I was afraid I'd fall in love with him.

Because in my past, falling in love meant giving up control.

It meant losing myself.

It meant pain.

But not this time.

This was the first time I was met with love that didn't need to fix me.

That didn't punish me for being slow.

That didn't ask me to shrink, prove, or explain.

It was just love.

Safe, steady love.

And the hardest part... was learning how to stay.

I See You

If you've ever turned away from someone who treated, you with care --

If you've felt your walls shoot up around people who were kind –

If you've ever mistaken peace for boredom, or safety for suspicion...

I want you to know this:

> You're not broken.
>
> You're not ungrateful.
>
> You're not pushing away the right person on purpose.
>
> You're healing.

And healing means *retraining* your heart to believe that love doesn't have to hurt.

It means learning that comfort is not a trap.

And slowness can be sacred.

Journal Reflection:

I am learning to stay when love is safe.

I am allowed to pause before letting someone in.

I am allowed to move slowly.

I am allowed to trust again – on *my* terms.

Love that is safe will never punish me for being careful.

It will not rush me.

It will not ask me to abandon myself.

I don't have to earn tenderness.

I only must believe I deserve it.

And I do.

Chapter 6:

The Fear of Healthy Love

We are not here to audition for love.

We are not meant to be constantly assessed, graded, or weighed.

We are not projects.

We are not puzzles to solve.

And love is not a test.

When you grow up being made to feel like you must be "good enough" to be kept, you carry that into every room you enter.

You overthink every word.

You anticipate disappointment.

You try to *earn your space* in someone's life – even if they've already told you they want you there.

Because somewhere deep down, you believe that your worth is conditional.

Maybe it started in childhood.

When praise only came after perfection.

When love was pulled away after a mistake.

When you were punished for having emotions.

Or when you were told, *"You're too much"* or *"You're not enough"* – and believed it.

So, you started to believe that love was something to *win.*

That if you just said the right thing...

Looked the right way...

Did all the right things...

Then maybe – *just maybe* – you'd finally be enough to stay.

That belief took root in me early.

I was always trying to earn love from my father.

Trying to be easy.

Trying to be agreeable.

Trying to succeed in ways he might finally notice.

I thought if I brought home good news, if I made him proud, if I did something impressive enough... he'd show up. He'd choose me.

He'd say, *"I'm proud of you."*

But the more I tried, the more invisible I felt.

No matter what I did, it never seemed to be enough.

And somewhere along the way, I internalized the lie that if I wasn't being chosen, it meant I wasn't trying hard enough.

It wasn't until I met someone who didn't need me to perform that I realized:

Love that is *real* doesn't ask you to keep proving your worth.

You are allowed to be loved as you are.

Without a test.

Without the performance.

Without constantly wondering if you're "doing it right."

I See You

If you've ever felt like love was a test you kept failing –

If you've shrunk yourself to be easier to love –

If you've bent until you broke trying to prove you're enough –

I want you to hear this:

You are not here to be earned.

You are not here to convince anyone to keep you.

The right people won't make you audition for their love.

They won't measure your worth by your silence, your achievements, or your ability to endure.

Love is not a prize for being perfect.

It is a *birthright.*

And you never had to earn what was always meant to be yours.

Journal Reflection:

I am not a test.

I am not a project.

I am not someone who has to prove their worth to be loved.

I do not have to shrink to fit someone's comfort.

I do not have to perform to be chosen.

I am allowed to be loved in my softness, in my silence, in my wholeness.

Love is not something I earn by being perfect.

It's something I receive because I am *human.*

And I am enough.

Just as I am.

Chapter 7:

When You've Only Known Survival

There is a version of love that doesn't leave you holding your breath.

But when you've only known survival...

Breathing feels unsafe.

Survival makes you hyper-aware.

You notice the shift in tone. The pause in a sentence. The silence after a text.

You play out worse-case scenarios before anything even happens.

You apologize before you know what you're apologizing for.

Because survival trained you to believe that the more alert you are, the safer you'll be.

It worked once. It *had* to.

When you were a child navigating unpredictable adults.

Or a partner monitoring their moods like weather patterns.

But survival doesn't turn off just because the danger is gone.

Even in love.

Even in peace.

Even when you're safe... your body still braces for impact.

And that's what no one tells you.

I still remember one of the first times my husband said he had a surprise for me.

Just a small thing – he was excited, kind, genuinely trying to do something sweet for me.

But the moment he said it, my stomach dropped.

My chest tightened.

My hands got shaky.

My mind spun with everything it *could* be – and none of it was good.

Because in my past, "surprises" weren't sweet.

They were punishments. Manipulations. Emotional setups.

They were followed by pain, humiliation, disappointment.

So, when someone I loved said, *"I've got something for you,"* my body prepared to flinch.

And even now, after years of healing and being loved well…

It still gets me sometimes.

He's learned not to build the suspense too much – because he knows it makes me spiral.

Not because he's done anything wrong, but because my body *remembers.*

That's what it means to be in recovery from survival mode.

You *want* to trust.

You *know* you're safe.

But your body is still catching up.

And healing means learning how to gently tell yourself:

This isn't then.

This isn't them.

This is now – and I am safe.

I See You

If your mind still jumps to worst-case scenarios...

If kindness makes you suspicious...

If your first instinct is to apologize for existing –

> You are not broken.

> You are not ungrateful.

> You are not overreacting.

You are someone who lived through chaos, and your brain is still trying to protect you.

> You survived.

> That's something to honor.

> And now, little by little...

You are learning what it means to live, not just *survive*.

Journal Reflection:

I am allowed to feel safe now.

I am no longer living in survival mode.

I don't have to anticipate pain just to feel prepared.

Love is not a trap.

Kindness is not a warning.

Surprises are not punishment.

This is a new chapter.

And I am learning, slowly and fully, that I am safe here.

My body can breathe now.

My heart can rest.

I am home.

Chapter 8:

Being Loved is Not the Same as Being Chosen

They told you they loved you.

But they left.

They showed up when it was convenient.

They disappeared when it mattered most.

That's not being chosen.

That's being kept *just enough* to stay unsure.

Some people love the idea of you.

They love how you make them feel.

They love what you give.

They love that you still pick up when they call.

But they never choose you. Not fully. Not consistently. Not in the way that counts. They love the version of you that makes their life easier. Not the one that asks for effort. Not the one that needs care.

That's not real love.

It's emotional convenience.

And for too long, we've been conditioned to believe it's enough.

My father only talked to me when it was convenient.

When he had time.

When it didn't interfere with the life, he'd built with someone else.

Sometimes he'd call from the bleachers at the games of the other children he was raising – kids who weren't even his biologically, but who got the version of him I always wanted. Who got the support, the cheering, the showing up.

And me?

I got the phone call during halftime.

I got the rushed conversations when his wife – finally – didn't need something.

I got the silence when things got hard.

And the dial tone when he didn't want to hear what I had to say.

I was on the back burner. The afterthought.

He chose me when it made him look good.

Like when I made it into a magazine for archery.

Then suddenly I was *his daughter.* A success story. A reason to brag.

But when I needed him…

When I just wanted a relationship…

When I wanted to *be chosen,* not just used —

He was gone.

He was a dad on paper. But only a father when it didn't interrupt his life. The life he *actually* wanted. Not the part that felt like the mistake — *me.*

And when that's the version of love you're raised on…

You start to believe that being chosen means being useful.

That being loved means being impressive.

That the only way to keep someone is to keep proving your worth.

But love that only shows up when it's convenient…

Isn't love.

It's access.

It's ego.

It's image.

You deserve more than being someone's "when I feel like it." You deserve to be *chosen*. On purpose. Every day.

I See You

If someone told you, that they loved you but never showed up —

If they only acknowledged you when it served them —

If you've spent your whole life feeling like you're easy to leave —

I want you to know this:

> Being loved is not the same as being chosen.
>
> Being kept around is not the same as being cared for.
>
> Being useful is not the same as being safe.

You don't have to settle for a love that only fits into someone else's schedule.

You don't have to be impressive to be worthy of showing up for.

> You deserve to be picked.
>
> Prioritized.
>
> Protected.
>
> You deserve a love that doesn't forget you.

Journal Reflection:

I am no longer settling for lover that comes and goes.

I am no longer clinging to people who only want me when it's easy.

I am worthy of being chosen fully.

Not just when it makes someone look good.

Not just when it fits into their plans.

I don't have to prove my value to be kept.

I am someone worth staying for.

And I no longer wait around for someone to remember that.

Part III:
Opening the Heart Again

Chapter 9:

The Body Remembers

Your heart might forgive.

Your mind might explain.

But your body?

Your body never forgets.

Trauma doesn't live in the past.

It lives in the body.

Even after the danger is gone –

After the abuser is blocked, after the relationship ends, after the apologies (or lack thereof) stop haunting your inbox – Your body still reacts.

The tension doesn't leave just because your brain understands. And healing doesn't happen just because you're *trying* to move forward.

My body has held trauma like a second skin.

Anxiety? It shows up like a storm out of nowhere. PTSD? Certain sounds, phrases, objects, even *gestures* can make my heart race.

I flinch easily – especially when someone raises their voice or walks in too quickly. Sometimes I zone out completely. Dissociation, like my body is still learning that it's *safe* to stay.

And the emotions?

When they come, they come *hard*.

Anger. Sadness. Fear.

Like old wounds that never really closed all the way.

My body learned early on that emotions were dangerous. That being "too much" got me in trouble. That my needs were a burden. That my *appearance* mattered more than my health. That being pleasing was safer than being present.

So of course, body image became a battlefield.

So of course, eating felt like control.

So of course, it felt safer to disappear than to be *seen*.

This is what trauma does.

It doesn't just hurt your past – it shapes how you move through the present.

And none of this makes you broken.

It makes you human.

A human who adapted to survive.

You were never too sensitive.

You weren't dramatic.

You were *in pain.*

And even now, if you find yourself overreacting, shutting down, struggling to stay connected –

I want you to know this:

It's okay.

Your body is not betraying you.

It's trying to protect you the only way it knows how.

You're just learning how to speak its language again.

I See You

If your body still tenses when nothing's wrong —

If you've ever been told you're "Too emotional," "too reactive," or "too sensitive" —

If you're exhausted from fighting your own nervous system…

I want you to hear this:

> Your body is not the enemy.

> It's the reason you're still here.

> It kept you alive when nothing else felt safe.

And now it's asking for something it's never had before —

> Gentleness.

> You don't have to *push through* anymore.

> You're allowed to slow down.

> You're allowed to rest.

You're allowed to relearn what safety feels like.

Journal Reflection:

I forgive my body for the ways it has carried my pain.

I forgive myself for not understanding its signals sooner.

I honor the ways my body has kept my safe.

The tension. The anxiety. The silence. The shutdowns.

I survived, because my body made sure I did.

Now, I am learning to live with it.

I am allowed to rest.

I am allowed to nourish.

I am allowed to feel safe inside myself.

I am no longer at war with the vessel that held me through the worst.

I am home here. I am healing.

Chapter 10:

It's Okay to Grieve What You Didn't Get

Some of the deepest grief you will ever feel…

Will be for the things you never received.

Not because you were unworthy.

But because someone else didn't know how to give them.

There are wounds created not by what happened… But by what *never* happened.

The comfort that wasn't offered. The reassurance that never came.

The safety that was never built for you.

The version of "love" that was always just out of reach – held like a prize you had to chase.

And it's okay to grieve that.

It's okay to grieve the birthday your father didn't remember.

The I'm sorry you never heard.

The way no one explained that your feelings weren't wrong.

That you were never too *much*.

It's okay to feel sadness, even years later, for the things your younger self needed *desperately* and never got.

My father has always been full of empty promises.

He used them like currency – dangling them in front of me to keep control, to feed his ego, to give the illusion of involvement.

But they never came through. Or if they did, it was hollow.

And the gifts?

They hurt more than not getting anything at all.

Not because I wanted something expensive.

But because I wanted something *thoughtful*. Something that said, *"I know you."*

Instead, they were impersonal.

Generic.

Sometimes just money in an envelope – proof that he didn't know me well enough to pick something I'd actually love.

Or worse… didn't care to.

And it stung.

Because even in the moments that were *supposed* to feel special, I felt unseen.

Those little moments – birthdays, holidays, milestones – they weren't about being spoiled. They were about being *known*. And when the people who are supposed to know you best don't even try –

That's a different kind of heartbreak.

So yes…

It's okay to grieve what you didn't get.

The hugs. The phone calls. The effort. The pride.

It's okay to grieve the love that was never personalized, never present, never protected.

Not because you're ungrateful.

Not because you're dramatic.

But because tour grief is telling the truth about what your younger self deserved.

I See You

If you've ever cried on your birthday for a reason, you couldn't explain…

If you've ever opened a gift and felt lonelier than if you got nothing at all…

It you've ever had to pretend something didn't hurt so you wouldn't feel like a burden…

I want you to know:

> You are not asking for too much.
>
> You were never wrong to want to be known.
>
> You were never wrong to want someone to *try.*
>
> You're allowed to grieve what never arrived.

You're allowed to mourn the version of childhood you didn't get to live.

Your grief is a sign of your capacity for love.

Not your weakness.

Journal Reflection:

I am allowed to grieve what I didn't get.

I am allowed to feel sad for the parts of me that were never held.

For the birthdays that felt like a formality.

For the gifts that reminded me I was unknown.

For the effort that never came.

I no longer must shrink my grief to make others comfortable.

I no longer must pretend it didn't hurt.

My grief is real.

My memories are valid.

My heart remembers because it was made for connection.

I can honor what was missing —

And still create the love I deserved all along.

Chapter 11:

How My Husband Loved Me into Believing Again

I didn't believe in real love anymore.

Not the safe kind. Not the quiet, steady kind.

But then he stayed.

Not because I asked him to –

But because he *wanted* to.

After everything I had survived, I didn't trust love.

Not easily.

Not fully.

Not without expecting it to hurt.

So, when my husband reached out to me, I pulled back.

I was guarded. Careful.

Not because I didn't like him – but because I *did*.

And liking someone had always come with consequences.

I had just started telling myself I was going to focus on my son.

On rebuilding. On healing.

I didn't want to be vulnerable again.

And he understood that.

He didn't push. He didn't guilt. He just stayed – quietly, patiently, kindly.

I had known my husband since preschool. We grew up in the same small town. Went to the same schools. We knew *of* each other, but never really *knew* each other.

Until he messaged me.

It was casual at first – just reconnecting.

But even through the screen, I could feel the difference.

He wasn't rushing me. He wasn't trying to charm me or corner me. He was simply there. Kind. Soft-spoken. Intentional.

Ans still, I hesitated.

Not because I didn't see his heart – but because I was terrified of what it would cost to trust again.

I turned him down. I told him I wasn't ready. That I was focusing on my son. That I didn't want to fall for someone just to lose myself again. And you know what he did?

He stayed.

Quietly. Respectfully. Steadily.

Not waiting to "win" me –

Just *willing* to be there, however I'd allow him to be.

We messaged. Every day. Nearly all day. Until six months passed. And one day – I agreed to meet him in person.

It wasn't a lightning bolt moment.

It was peace.

It was ease.

It was everything love had never felt like before.

He didn't love me with conditions. He didn't try to fix me. He didn't panic when I flinched or pulled away.

He just *stayed*.

He listened.

He made space.

Even before he knew my full story, he treated me like someone worthy of gentleness. And after he *did* learn the details?

He never turned away.

He reminded me – over and over again, without words – that love doesn't hurt to be real.

That I don't have to earn it. That I can mess up, speak up, take up space...

And he'll still be there.

Not because he *has* to.

But because he *wants* to.

And that's when I started to believe again.

I See You

If you've ever wondered whether real love exists…

If you've ever thought, you were too broken to be loved gently…

If you've ever flinched at the idea of someone seeing the real, you —

I want you to know:

> There is a kind of love that won't flinch when you tell the truth.

> There is a kind of love that doesn't try to fix you — only hold you.

> There is a kind of love that will sit quietly beside your pain, not rush it away.

And the love *is not a fantasy*.

> It's possible.

> It's real.

> And you *deserve* it.

Journal Reflection:

I am not too much.

I am not too broken.

I am not too hard to love.

I am learning that love doesn't have to hurt to be real.

I don't have to earn tenderness.

I don't have to perform to feel safe.

I am allowed to rest in love.

I am allowed to trust someone who stays.

I am allowed to receive the very thing I once gave away too easily.

Real love sees me.

Holds me.

Stays with me.

And I am finally learning to believe it's mine to keep.

Chapter 12:

Triggers Aren't Proof You're Broken

A trigger is not a flaw.

It's a message.

A memory wrapped in protection.

A part of you saying,

"This feels too familiar. Please be careful."

People often talk about "healing" like it means never being triggered again. But healing isn't erasing the wound – it's learning how to care for it when it aches.

Triggers can show up in a hundred different ways. A phrase. A tone of voice. A certain silence.

Even being loved gently can be triggering – because it doesn't match what you were taught love looked like.

Sometimes you shut down.

Sometimes you snap.

Sometimes you cry over something small and don't know why.

And that's not a failure.

It's not weakness.

It's your nervous system doing exactly what it was trained to do: *protect you.*

So many of my triggers catch me completely off guard.

A man walking behind me.

A glance over my shoulder.

A sound I can't quite place.

Even if it's harmless — *especially* when it is — my body doesn't wait to be sure. It reacts.

It doesn't matter that I "know better."

That it's probably nothing.

That I'm "safe now."

Because my nervous system doesn't live in logic — it lives in memory.

There are weapons I can't even look at in a store. Knitting needles. Shotguns. They were once used against me once —

Not always physically, but emotionally. Symbolically. Threats. Intimidation. Control.

And now?

I can be walking through a store and suddenly feel like I can't breathe – without even knowing why.

Until it clicks.

My eyes avoid an aisle.

My heart raced when I wasn't even aware I was holding something inside.

This is what trauma does. It writes fear into the spaces you no longer want to occupy.

And the shame of that?

Of reacting to something "normal," "every day," "harmless?"

That shame is what we *must* release.

Because your reaction isn't proof that you're broken – It's proof that you *survived* something that changed you.

I See You

If you've ever felt ashamed of your triggers —

If you've ever told yourself, you were being ridiculous or dramatic —

If you've ever walked through a public space and felt your chest tighten for "no reason" —

I want you to know:

> You are not weak.
>
> You are not overreacting.
>
> You are not broken.
>
> You are a person whose body remembers pain.

And who is learning, one moment at a time, how to live beyond it.

Journal Reflection:

My triggers do not make me broken.

They are echoes of pain I didn't choose.

I will stop apologizing for the ways my body
remembers.

I will stop shaming myself for needing time, space,
and breath.

I am not failing – I am feeling.

I am learning to meet my fear with softness.

I am learning to stay present even when the past
tries to pull me back.

I am safe now.

I am healing.

I am worthy of gentleness.

My body is not my enemy.

It is my protector.

And I am learning to trust it again.

Chapter 13:

Love That Doesn't Hurt

Love that doesn't hurt doesn't mean love without difficulty.

It means love that doesn't make you question your worth.

It means love that doesn't weaponize your fears.

It means being able to breathe – fully – in the presence of someone who holds your heart.

I used to believe that love was supposed to feel like chaos. Like holding your breath and hoping it wouldn't be the day everything exploded.

I thought love was something you had to earn – and then keep proving you were worthy of.

That it was conditional. Fleeting. A performance.

And for a long time, I accepted pain as a natural part of love.

When you've only ever known love that leaves you anxious, small, or afraid, real love feels foreign. Gentle love feels suspicious. Calm feels dangerous. You're always waiting for the other shoe to drop – because in your experience, it always did.

But then I found love that didn't hurt.

And it terrified me.

Because when someone sees you fully – your brokenness, your softness, your shar edges – and doesn't flinch or run… it makes you question everything you were taught.

Love that doesn't hurt doesn't mean love is perfect.

It means love that doesn't punish.

Love that doesn't manipulate.

Love that doesn't leave you questioning your value.

My husband has never once made me earn his affection.

He doesn't disappear when I cry. He doesn't roll his eyes when I'm overwhelmed. He doesn't twist my fears into weapons.

He listens.

He stays.

He chooses me.

And perhaps the hardest part of this journey was learning to believe I was worth that kind of love. That I could be safe. That love could be steady and kind. That love could heal.

It's strange to say that meeting my husband was also the beginning of the end of my relationship with my father. But in many ways, it was.

Because for the first time in my life, I saw how a man *should* treat a woman.

How a father *should* care for his daughter.

How love, at its core, is not about power – but about presence.

My husband never tried to fix me.

He didn't try to save me.

He simply stood beside me and let me borrow his strength until I could stand on my won. He believed in me long before I believed in myself.

And that kind of love?

It holds up a mirror to all the love you *thought* you had but never truly did.

It reveals every crack. Every moment you convinced yourself that pain was normal. That neglect was your fault. That love only came when you were perfect, quiet, or convenient.

My husband never forced me to choose between him and my father.

But loving him helped me see what I had accepted for far too long.

And once you know what real love feels like...

It becomes impossible to keep lying to yourself about the kind that hurts.

There's something quietly revolutionary about being loved well.

It softens the parts of you that have lived in survival mode. It makes space for the pieces you used to hide. And slowly, it teaches you that you don't have to live guarded anymore.

At first, I struggled to trust it.

Kindness felt like a trick. Consistency made me nervous. Being seen without being judged left me exposed in a way I wasn't used to.

But day by day, my husband didn't flinch.

He didn't run.

He didn't shame me for how long it took to believe I was safe.

Instead, he helped me rewrite what I thought love had to be. He helped me unlearn that love was something to be earned. He helped me recognize that I wasn't "too much," and I was never a burden.

He helped me see that the love I had accepted in the past was never love at all.

And that realization – that I could be fully loved *as I am* – That gave me the courage to walk away from every version of "love" that hurt.

I See You

I don't know your story, but I know what it's like to question whether love is worth the pain.

I know what it's like to crave affection and fear it at the same time.

To wonder if real love even exists – and if it does, whether someone like you deserves it.

Let me tell you something that I wish someone would've told me years ago:

> You do.
>
> You are worthy of a love that doesn't ask you to shrink.
>
> A love that sees your scars and stays anyway.
>
> A love that grows with you, not against you.
>
> Love that doesn't hurt *does* exist.
>
> And you don't have to settle for anything less.

Real love might not always be flashy or perfect.

It won't always have grand gestures or flawless days.

> But real love *shows up*.

It looks like someone remembering the things that matter to you –

> Even the small ones.

It sounds like safety in their voice when you're spiraling.

It feels like stillness when your world is anything but still.

Real love holds your hand through the hard.

It lets you exhale.

It helps you heal – not because it fixes everything, but because it never asks you to carry it all alone.

Journal Reflection:

"You're not too broken to be loved gently."

Real love doesn't hurt to hold.

Real love feels like peace, not panic.

It may come quietly, but it will never confuse you.

You are worthy of love that makes you feel safe.

Of love that doesn't require you to become smaller
to keep it.

Let that be your new standard.

Chapter 14:

Reclaiming Intimacy

I didn't know how much my body still remembered.

Not just the pain, but the panic.

The instinct to flinch, freeze, or disappear.

The way my chest tightened at the thought of being touched, even by someone I trusted.

Sometimes it felt like my skin didn't belong to me.

Like I had to earn my right to feel safe inside it again.

I wanted to be close – but closeness didn't always feel good. It felt dangerous. Or worse... expected.

I thought I had healed until I tried to let someone love me again. And suddenly, I realize how many pieces of me were still afraid.

In trauma, intimacy shifts.

It stops being sacred – and starts being something feared. Or worse, something you disconnect from entirely.

That's what I did.

For a while, intimacy became something detached – almost transactional.

Hookups felt safer than real connection. Because there was nothing to lose if it was empty from the start. If I didn't let anyone get too close, I couldn't be hurt.

And yet, I was still hurting.

The truth is, when your body has been violated, it becomes harder to hear your heart.

I told myself, I was in control, but my heart still wanted love. Not convenience. Not numbness. Not validation from strangers.

I wanted to be chosen. Known. Safe.

But I didn't know it that kind of intimacy was even possible anymore.

Then I met my husband.

He never once made me feel like I owed him my body. He didn't view intimacy as a right or an expectation. He saw it as something we built together – with trust, with care, and with time.

And for the first time, I didn't feel used.

I felt wanted.

He was gentle. Vocal. Patient.

He asked questions. He gave me space. He never rushed. He reminded me – again and again – that *I* was sacred.

That this part of our relationship wasn't about control or obligation. It was about connection. Shared joy. Trust.

And that… was something my brain didn't know how to process at first. Because safety and pleasure had never existed in the same sentence for me before.

But his love helped retrain my nervous system.

He helped me breathe through the fear.

He reminded me that my body still belonged to *me*.

And slowly… gently… I began to believe it.

I See You

If no one has ever said this to you, let me say it now:

> You are not broken for finding intimacy hard.

> You are not cold or distant or too damaged.

> You are healing.

> What happened to you wasn't your fault.

And what your body learned to do to survive – the shutting down, the disconnecting, the fear – that wasn't failure.

> That was protection.

> But you deserve more than just survival.

> You deserve to feel safe *and* desired.

You deserve to reclaim every part of yourself that was taken, silenced, or made to feel shameful.

> Intimacy can be rebuilt.

> It doesn't happen overnight.

But with someone safe – or even just with yourself – it can become something beautiful again.

> It can be yours again.

You are still worthy of soft touches and slow kisses.

> Of being held without expectation.

> Of closeness that heals, not harms.

Let that be the standard from now on.

Journal Reflection:

"My body is mine again. My healing is not linear — bit it is sacred."

I do not owe anyone access to me.

I am not damaged goods.

I am allowed to take my time.

When I choose intimacy, it will be on my terms.

When I allow someone in, it will be because they've earned my trust.

I am not defined by what happened to me.

I am worthy of love, of safety, and of passion that honors my healing.

Chapter 15:

For the One Who's Still Afraid to Love Again

I used to say I didn't want to fall in love again. But that wasn't the truth.

I wanted to love. I just didn't want to lose myself doing it. I didn't want to be fooled, again. I didn't want to give someone all the softest parts of me, just to watch them be thrown away.

I was terrified – not of love itself, but what I thought love always turned into.

Hurt.

Betrayal.

Disappointment.

So, I stayed alone for a while. Not because I wanted to be – but because I was afraid that letting someone in meant losing the safety I had finally built.

I didn't know yet that the right love wouldn't tear my walls down. It would ask permission to walk through the door.

I see you – the one who's still afraid to love again.

You're not cold.

You're not unlovable.

You're just tired of hurting.

You've given love every chance it asked for, only to watch it fade, shift, or destroy the parts of you that were never meant to be broken. And now? You're afraid to try again. You don't want to be someone's lesson or steppingstone. Not again.

I get it.

Because I've been there.

I've stared at my phone, wondering if it was safer to never respond. I've pulled away from a kind hand, convinced it would eventually turn cruel. I've seen red flags and told myself they were "just shadows." I've mistaken adrenaline for love, control for protection, silence for peace.

And then I met someone who didn't try to fix me – but gave me space to heal.

Someone who never pushed – just stayed close enough for me to realize that maybe, just maybe… not everyone wanted to hurt me.

It took time.

It took tears. It took unlearning. It took believing that I was allowed to be loved in a way that felt good, safe, and soft.

And you are too.

You are allowed to take your time.

You are allowed to ask questions.

You are allowed to love again – slowly, gently, and on your terms.

Not everyone is your past.

Not everyone will take what you give and leave you empty.

There are people who will stay.

People who will listen. People who will love you in a way that doesn't feel like a fight.

Let them.

Let *you*.

Because love is not the enemy.

Pain disguised as love was.

Journal Reflection:

"You don't have to rush. Healing is still healing, even if you're scared."

I know you're afraid to love again.

But that fear is not weakness — its wisdom earned.

And still…

You're not too broken.

You are not too complicated.

You are not too much.

There is someone who will hold your heart like it's holy — because it is.

You don't have to be fully healed to be fully loved.

You've got this.

Once brave moment at a time.

From My Heart to Yours

Dear Reader,

If you've made it to this page, I want to thank you – not just for reading, but for *feeling* your way through this with me.

This book was never just about my story. It was about what happens when pain no longer gets the final word. When survivors rise. When we learn to trust again. To love again. To *breathe* again.

I know what it feels like to question everything – your worth, your voice, your ability to ever feel safe in love again. I know what it's like to carry wounds that the world can't see but that you feel every day. And I know how lonely it can be to wonder if anyone else *gets it.*

But I want you to know… you're not alone.

I wrote this book because I needed someone to say the words I couldn't find back then.

I needed someone to show me that healing is possible. That soft love still exists. That the girl who was once afraid to be touched, to be known, to be *seen,* could still become a woman who is cherished – not despite her pain, but because of her courage.

So, if this book helped you feel a little less alone, if it reminded you that your past does not disqualify you from your future, then I hope you'll carry that truth with you.

You are worthy.

You are capable.

You are still healing – and that's beautiful.

And one day, if you haven't already, you'll look back and realize you didn't just survive.

You reclaimed your story.

With all my heart,

- Genevieve McPartlin-Bryant